The Decision Guide

for

Nonprofit Boards

Lisa Dahmus

Decision Publishing
www.DecisionPublishing.com

DEDICATION

In memory of my grandfather Joseph Dahmus,
who through his example inspired
me to write books.

CONTENTS

PREFACE

I began writing the *Decision Guide* when I was in a master's of business administration program at the University of Michigan. There I met Professor Frank Yates, who wrote *Decision Management*, which analyzes decision making in the corporate setting. I was excited when I read his book and took his class because I believed his insights could be applied to nonprofit boards.

The *Decision Guide* leverages his ideas along with my experience working with nonprofit boards to provide a straightforward, practical guide to improving your board's decision making and meeting management. The eight issues described in this book form a powerful framework from which boards can develop and continuously improve. These issues are also the basis for the offerings provided by the Customized Interactions consulting practice, an organization focused on increasing board effectiveness.

CHAPTER 1
INTRODUCTION

Nonprofit boards are responsible for delivering the organization's mission, acquiring funding, hiring the chief executive, structuring and overseeing the committees necessary to run the organization, responding to crises, and addressing countless other tasks. What do these responsibilities have in common? They all involve decision making. In fact, almost everything boards do boils down to decision making. On the surface, decision making might seem easy, but it is not as simple as it seems. The consequences of poor decision making are many, from wasted time to destructive conflict to financial and legal issues. Improvement in this area can help strengthen any organization, while dysfunctional decision making can ruin the most well-meaning charities. With such dire consequences possible, the importance of recognizing an issue is clear, but how do you do so? Fortunately, early warning signs exist. The list below provides some symptoms. Take a moment to reflect on the questions. Do any of these describe your board?

- Does your board repeat the same discussion meeting after meeting?
- Do board members avoid difficult discussions during meetings?
- Do you experience a high level of unproductive conflict during meetings?

- Is the relationship between the board and staff tense?
- Do you feel you never have enough money to run your programs?

If you answered yes to any of these questions, your board might have developed poor decision-making processes, and it is worth your time to reflect on areas for improvement now.

Poor decision making can cripple or even ruin an organization. For example, one nonprofit organization well known in the community for providing excellent athletic programs for elementary and middle school children desired to build on its success by creating an after-school program for high school students. The board chair, Jim,[1] recalled, "The community was really pulling for the program. Numerous times I would be at the gym or in the grocery store, and someone from the community would stop me and ask when we planned to get the program going. During those moments, I would ask myself, 'Why hadn't we started it yet?'"

Board members brought up the topic often during meetings, and the group became increasingly impatient to take action and make the idea a reality. But not everyone was supportive. A couple of board members opposed the idea because it would require another gymnasium that would be expensive to rent. Unfortunately, these board members were less vocal than the majority and often voiced their concerns behind closed doors after the meeting.

Finally, during one particularly emotional meeting in which Jim relayed another plea from a community member to add the program,

---

1 In all of the examples presented in this book, board member names and identifying information about specific boards have been modified to protect the board's anonymity.

the board made the official decision to pull the trigger and implement the program. Jill, who was usually quiet during meetings, expressed her frustration. "I just have a bad feeling about this," she said. Some of the other members reassured her it would work out.

After a few months of operating the program, the number of clients enrolled was much lower than the board expected. Many of the parents who had expressed interest did not follow through and register their children for the program, partly because the organization implemented the program in the middle of the school year when many students were already on established sports teams. Unfortunately, it became painfully obvious that the organization did not have the client base or funds to sustain the program. As a result, the program was discontinued, disappointing many people in the community and demoralizing the staff and board.

So why did this decision fail? The board and particularly the board chair, Jim, were so excited about making the program successful that they relied on faith that they could make it happen. They did not seek out and process dissenting opinions and did not conduct an adequate financial and market analysis before deciding to implement the new program. Had the board members carefully analyzed the finances and confronted the reality of the situation, they would have realized that before implementing the program, they needed to develop a plan to acquire additional funds. After the failed attempt to add the new program, the board and staff became reluctant to try again. This is unfortunate, because I believe the board could have successfully implemented the program if they had thoroughly analyzed the situation and worked together to develop a plan.

Even if the decisions your board makes do not jeopardize the future of the organization, your decision-making processes might be time consuming and frustrating, diverting resources away from other activities that warrant attention. The *Decision Guide* is designed to give boards a framework for reflecting on and improving their decision-making processes to ensure they govern the organization in the most effective way and create the most positive experience possible for staff and board members alike. So what does a good decision-making process look and feel like? Here are some reflections from board members.

Our new board chair pushes us to review information prior to meetings. I am very busy, so at first I was annoyed, but soon I realized how much more we accomplished during meetings. I enjoy the discussions we have in our meetings much more now that we are all prepared.

After a lengthy discussion of the new program we wanted to implement, my board decided to postpone the implementation of the program for six months. We were disappointed, but we all knew it was the right thing to do. We are more resolved than ever to do the work to secure the client base we need to make the program successful.

In our board retreat, we developed a comprehensive fundraising strategy, and before we left, we assigned action items to one another and committed to completing them by the next meeting. I left the meeting feeling confident we would follow through and raise the money we committed to.

Our committees are active. We meet monthly and get a lot done outside of meetings, so we can use the meeting time for issues that need thorough discussion.

The above situations illustrate the outcomes of good decision making. On an emotional level, good decision making is energizing, satisfying, and even fun. Trust and open dialogue provide a foundation for effective decision making, and well-defined group processes support it. If your board has clearly defined roles and responsibilities, follows an agenda, and records and follows through on action items, you are on the right track. But even if your board does these things, there is always room for improvement. In addition, as board membership changes, your group could slip into bad habits.

Good decision making may seem deceptively simple, but even effective processes have a way of breaking down when people are under stress. This guide describes eight issues that derail even the most well-meaning boards and provides simple tools for avoiding these pitfalls.

CHAPTER 2
HOW TO USE THE DECISION GUIDE

The *Decision Guide* is designed to provide you with personal insight and practical tools you can use immediately to enhance your board's performance and your own satisfaction as a board member.

The guide analyzes eight issues that impact many boards. In the discussion of the issues, tools are introduced to help your board make the right decisions (Chapter 3), secure the necessary inputs (Chapter 4), and make and implement decisions effectively (Chapter 5).

You will get the most out of this guide if you consider the issue discussions from the perspective of your board. As you read about each issue, ask yourself the following questions:

- What does my board do well in this area?
- What is my board struggling with?
- Which tools might help us increase our effectiveness?

A series of reflection questions are provided at the end of each issue discussion to enable you to record your insights and further reflect on how the recommendations and tools might help your board.

The issues described in this guide are illustrated using examples of real boards although board member names and identifying information about specific boards have been modified to protect the board's anonymity.

The worksheets presented during the issue discussions are completed based on the experiences of real boards. A full set of blank worksheets is provided in the appendix.

Chapter 6 provides practical tips for how to implement the tools presented in this guide. Chapter 7 provides additional resources including books, organizations, and other support available to your board.

CHAPTER 3
MAKE THE RIGHT DECISIONS

Issue 1—Clarify Roles

The Issue

Does your board ever make decisions that the staff should make? Or does your board fail to make decisions, thinking that the responsibility lies with someone else, usually the staff? When boards do this, they have not properly defined roles and responsibilities, and the following issue is likely to occur:

> *Boards spend excessive amounts of time debating issues that are the staff's responsibility.*

When board members do not have a clear understanding of what their responsibilities really are, they may resort to addressing what seem to be the most pressing issues or be tempted to make the types of decisions they are most comfortable making. For example, I witnessed one board spending valuable meeting time discussing which long-distance carrier to use. After the discussion, Julie, the chief executive, pulled me aside and exclaimed, "Do they not trust us to do our job?" The staff should make this type of decision. When boards make decisions that belong to the staff, they are micromanaging, and this has costs. As this example highlights, micromanaging can cause staff members to feel second-guessed or not trusted. Micromanaging also takes time away from the more strategic decisions that are necessary for the effective governance of the organization.

Issue 1 does not always involve the board making staff decisions. Sometimes boards mistakenly believe that someone else should make a particular decision, and thus they take no action. For instance, one board of an agency funded by large government grants and a variety of smaller fund-raising events and programs failed to develop a comprehensive fund-raising strategy. During one meeting, board member Karen commented, "We have not had a fund-raising event in a while. I wonder if the staff has anything planned." This particular staff did organize periodic fund-raising activities, but they were not equipped to set the overarching strategy necessary to provide the revenue streams to sustain the organization. Because one of the board's major responsibilities is that of ensuring that the organization has the necessary resources, this board should have proactively developed a fund-raising strategy and empowered the staff to implement the portions of the plan that fell under their purview.

Addressing the Issue

Issue 1 alerts boards to the importance of understanding and clarifying roles and responsibilities. A necessary first step toward avoiding these problems is for board members to have a clear understanding of the problems and issues they should be considering. Boards often fall prey to making inappropriate decisions because they do not think about or do not agree upon the division of responsibilities between board and staff. Stated simply, the role of the board is to set strategy and policy, while the role of the staff is to implement the strategy and policy set by the board. When boards neglect governance activities and focus more on day-to-day management, they run the risk of becoming counterproductive micromanagers.

It is important to note that board and staff responsibilities might overlap if the organization has a small staff. One organization I work with, a dance school in the Northeast, has one full-time staff member. The board of this organization manages the accounting and bookkeeping activities and even does some property maintenance. In an organization with a larger staff, these tasks would be a staff responsibility.

Keep in mind the following key points from the discussion so far: (1) boards must not neglect governance activities, and (2) the board and staff must work together to clearly define and document the division of responsibilities to ensure no key activities are neglected. This division will vary based on the size of the organization, the number of staff members, and other factors.

Governing the organization involves setting strategy and ensuring the staff has the resources necessary to implement the strategy. Managing involves decisions and activities focused on realizing the strategy. To illustrate, some activities the board should typically avoid include selecting which vendor to use, purchasing equipment and supplies, and hiring staff members (except for hiring the chief executive). If you would like a more detailed discussion of board responsibilities, *Ten Basic Responsibilities of Nonprofit Boards*, by Richard T. Ingram, is a good resource.

If board members become involved in activities outside of their basic responsibilities, they waste valuable time they could otherwise spend strategizing and planning for the organization's future. Micromanaging board members also risk alienating staff members. The board I described earlier routinely became involved in management activities. The discussion about the long-distance carrier was one of many examples. When I was brought in to consult with the board, a very tense relationship existed between the board and staff as a result of this micromanaging.

So how specifically could you work to ensure your board is making the decisions it needs to be making and not micromanaging? I recommend simply spending time during a board meeting or board retreat to discuss, clarify, and document the board and staff roles and responsibilities, with a special focus on the decisions board and staff members should be making. In the meeting, one possible format would be to ask each member to reflect on the discussions the board has had and the resulting decisions the board has made over the last year. After giving members some time to reflect individually, discuss and capture a list of the decisions. Then, for each decision, evaluate whether it is a governance or management decision. If it is a management decision, probe further to understand why the board made a management decision. Then evaluate whether the board should be making such decisions. Based on this evaluation, identify what the board is doing effectively and note any opportunities for improvement. Before leaving the meeting, commit to making the changes that the group identified. Document the process so this can serve as a baseline for you to gauge improvements.

The micromanaging school board mentioned earlier used the Role Clarification Reflection process to evaluate their past decisions. In doing so, they realized that more than half of their decisions in the previous year involved areas that belonged to the staff. This was a real eye-opener for the board and validating for Julie, the chief executive. I remember Bill, one of the board members, came up to me after the meeting and said, "When I see it in black-and-white, I understand why Julie has accused us of micromanaging." Table 1 provides the worksheet they completed for one of the decisions they identified as a management decision. A blank worksheet is provided in the appendix.

TABLE 1. Example Role Clarification Reflection

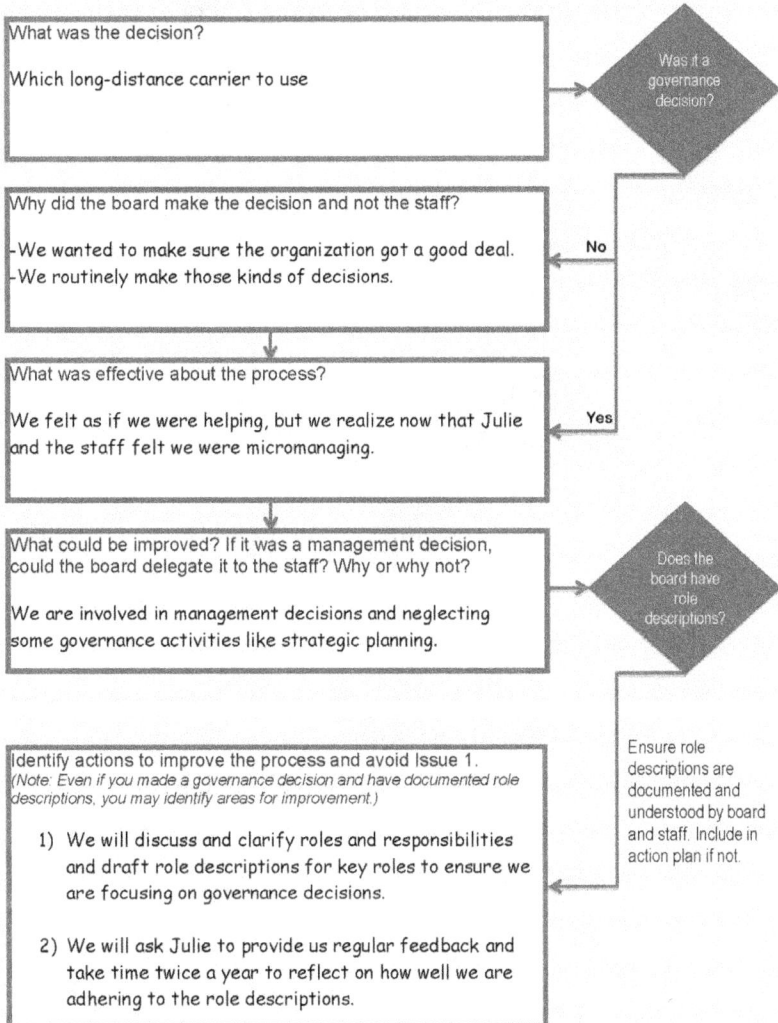

What was the decision?

Which long-distance carrier to use

Was it a governance decision?

Why did the board make the decision and not the staff?

-We wanted to make sure the organization got a good deal.
-We routinely make those kinds of decisions.

No

What was effective about the process?

We felt as if we were helping, but we realize now that Julie and the staff felt we were micromanaging.

Yes

What could be improved? If it was a management decision, could the board delegate it to the staff? Why or why not?

We are involved in management decisions and neglecting some governance activities like strategic planning.

Does the board have role descriptions?

Identify actions to improve the process and avoid Issue 1.
(Note: Even if you made a governance decision and have documented role descriptions, you may identify areas for improvement.)

1) We will discuss and clarify roles and responsibilities and draft role descriptions for key roles to ensure we are focusing on governance decisions.

2) We will ask Julie to provide us regular feedback and take time twice a year to reflect on how well we are adhering to the role descriptions.

Ensure role descriptions are documented and understood by board and staff. Include in action plan if not.

The Role Clarification Reflection builds trust and paves the way for a board to have open dialogue and productive conflict. How does it achieve these ends? First it promotes open dialogue about group functioning allowing the group to surface points of contention or ambiguity. Second, it sets clear expectations for how the group will operate. In Julie's example, the activity helped Julie express her concerns and helped the board members understand the impact their actions had on her. Going forward, if the board slips into past behavior patterns, Julie can remind them of the discussions they had during the Role Clarification Reflection as a means to hold them accountable.

If a board does not have descriptions documenting board and chief executive roles and responsibilities, members should take the time to develop them. Julie's board did not have them, so after completing the Role Clarification Reflection, her board worked together to create draft role descriptions for the key roles. Then they met with a larger group including key staff members to ensure they had considered all viewpoints. After updating the descriptions, the board included them in the standard operating procedures of the board. The board also decided to take time twice a year to reflect on their recent decisions to ensure they remain true to their documented role descriptions. Julie called me up six months after the process and said the relationships between the board and staff had improved greatly as a result of clarifying and documenting roles and responsibilities.

Issue 1 Reflection

The following questions give you an opportunity to reflect on how *Issue 1–Lack of role clarity* affects your board and how the recommendations discussed in this section could help your board clarify roles.

- What insights did you gain through reading this section?

- Does your board clearly understand their roles and responsibilities? Does your board have written role descriptions?

- Does your board neglect any governance activities? If so, which ones and why?

- Has your board ever made decisions that belong to the staff? If so, why and what was the impact?

- Could any of the recommendations presented in this section help your board? If so, which ones?

Issue 2—Operate Proactively

The Issue

Even when board members clearly understand their roles and responsibilities and limit their decisions to these areas, they may not be making the "right" decisions. Why? They might be missing key opportunities entirely. This happens when boards operate in a reactive mode and do not proactively consider the decisions on which they should focus.

Take a moment to reflect on the following example. One board has not updated their strategic plan for over five years. Several board members regularly comment on the need for an updated plan, but no one has taken the initiative to begin the process. Instead, the board continues to meet monthly and make decisions without the guidance of a comprehensive strategic plan. In this case, the board should make decisions regarding the development of a strategic plan, such as who should draft the plan and by when. But the board has failed to make these decisions.

This example may sound similar to the example in the previous section about the board that failed to develop a comprehensive fund-raising strategy. These situations produce the same result but stem from a different root cause. Issue 1 occurs when boards have not defined their responsibilities appropriately and thus fail to make the necessary governance decisions. Issue 2 results when boards do not have processes to ensure they are proactively identifying the decisions they need to make. In both cases, the boards failed to make necessary governance decisions. In the fund-raising example, the board believed the responsibility belonged to the staff, and in the strategic plan example, the board was operating in a reactive mode. In either situation, the following outcome is likely:

Boards are sometimes blindsided because they have failed
to discuss or identify an issue early enough.

Catching problems when they are small can prevent catastrophes from developing later. For instance, one educational agency relied on a government grant for the majority of its funds. Budget cuts jeopardized the future of the funds. Over several years, the agency was constantly facing the risk of losing the grant funds. Throughout this period, the board continued to discuss how to ensure they met the grant requirements, but no one thought to discuss the possibility of finding an alternative revenue stream in the event that the government cut the grant. Unfortunately, one year the inevitable happened, and the government eliminated the grant. The board called an emergency session to discuss the crisis. Emotion was high. One board member commented on how powerless he felt. Another, almost in tears, exclaimed, "What will we tell the parents?" As humans, our best thinking and creativity do not come when we are in a state of fear. Failing to proactively identify a decision they needed to make forced the board to make difficult decisions in crisis mode. Instead of having several years to explore funding sources, the board had only several months to determine how to find alternative funding.

The discussion so far has focused on boards failing to identify critical decisions. But Issue 2 could take another form when boards make decisions they should not be making. Doing so takes time away from work the board should be doing. For instance, one board spent thirty minutes of meeting time debating which flavors of ice cream to serve at a charity picnic. Such a discussion should occur outside of the main board meeting at a committee meeting, because it takes time away from other critical decisions. These kinds of discussions are symptoms of operating in a reactive mode. Why? Because they are typically not planned. The tools described in the following section are designed to help boards operate proactively. Throughout the book, other tools will be presented to focus discussions and make the best use of time in board meetings.

Addressing the Issue

The previous examples show that failing to make decisions about the right things can waste time or, worse, create a situation in which your board is blindsided when small issues turn into big problems. So how can you ensure you are making decisions about the right things? The first step, addressed in the Issue 1 discussion, is to clearly define roles and responsibilities in order to avoid making decisions that others should make. In addition to clearly defining roles, board members must be on the alert and speak up if any of these unproductive discussions occur. The meeting facilitation tools described in the Issue 7 discussion will also help.

The second step toward making decisions about the right things is to identify proactively decisions that should be made, and schedule time to discuss those items. The board can achieve this by conducting periodic brainstorming sessions and using a new tool, the Agenda Planning Calendar, to schedule decision-related discussions.

We will start by considering the brainstorming process, a structured time for board members to consider potential decisions so as to avoid Issue 2. A board can run a brainstorming session in a variety of ways. Each board should design a process that is appropriate for their group and goals. The next paragraphs provide some ideas.

Any brainstorming activity should encourage board members to consider potential issues facing the organization or opportunities that could strengthen it. A useful framework for doing this is a SWOT Analysis. A SWOT Analysis categorizes factors facing the organization in terms of *strengths, weaknesses, opportunities,* or *threats.* It is one step in developing the organization's strategic plan. A completed strategic plan can guide future decisions the organization should make and outline how those decisions interconnect to ensure the agency delivers its mission and ultimately achieves its vision. For a step-by-step guide to developing a strategic plan, see the Customized Interactions website at www.CustomizedInteractions.com.

To conduct a SWOT analysis, first reflect on and then list the agency's strengths and weaknesses. Strengths are internal factors that contribute to the agency's success while weaknesses are internal factors that hinder the effectiveness of the agency. Some examples follow:

- **Strength**—Several of our teachers have highly specialized skills that no other educational organization in the community possesses.
- **Strength**—Our agency is well-known and respected in the community.
- **Weakness**—Our facilities are inadequate for the increasing client base.
- **Weakness**—We have lost a number of staff members and are unable to adequately staff our current programs.

Next, consider the opportunities and threats facing the organization. These are external factors that influence the organization's success, including the economic, social, political, and legal situation as well as available technology. Opportunities could potentially add to the success of the agency while threats could potentially hinder the success of the agency. Some examples follow:

- **Opportunity**—We have established collaborative relationships with the local college that help us enhance our fine-arts program.
- **Opportunity**—A large corporation has moved to our small town. Parents will be enrolling their children in schools, so we have an opportunity to increase enrollment.
- **Threat**—The economy has slowed down, so we are losing clients.
- **Threat**—Technological changes have made our current software obsolete.

After generating the list of strengths, weaknesses, opportunities, and threats, identify potential decisions by considering the following:

- Should any of the agency's strengths be given particular attention? For instance, if the agency has teachers with highly specialized skills that no other agency possesses, the board may consider reaching out to other organizations whose clients might be interested in participating in programs with those teachers.
- Should any of the agency's weaknesses be addressed? For instance, an agency with inadequate facilities might need to begin discussions to decide whether to add another building.
- Should any of the opportunities facing the organization be exploited? For instance, the board might decide to partner with the local college to offer a new program.

- Should actions be taken to address the threats? For instance, the board of a private school might discuss options to lower tuition because of the slow economy.

A SWOT brainstorming session stimulates creativity and gets ideas on the table. During the brainstorming session, each person has the opportunity to voice his or her ideas, and all input is recorded for the group to see. After all members have provided their input, the group should reach consensus on critical decisions that need to be made. The group can then record these decisions on an Agenda Planning Calendar (described in the next paragraph) for discussion at future meetings. The last chapter outlines a step-by-step brainstorming process that your board can use.

The Agenda Planning Calendar, when used along with a brainstorming process, is key to designing and conducting effective board meetings. Board members prepare this document once a year at a board retreat, including in it major activities that they will conduct and topics they will discuss at future board meetings. At each board meeting, they update it to include new agenda items identified through the course of the meeting and delete any irrelevant items.

During meetings, it serves as a means to keep the meeting on track. If a participant raises an idea that needs to be considered and discussed, the board should note it in a bucket list and then include it on the Agenda Planning Calendar. This approach focuses the board and prevents the discussion of inappropriate issues (such as the flavor of ice cream to serve!).

The Agenda Planning Calendar reminds the group to engage in the brainstorming sessions discussed above. Table 2, an example Agenda Planning Calendar is only partially filled out and shows an agenda item, *Brainstorm Potential Decisions*, planned for the March, July, and November meetings.

TABLE 2. Example Agenda Planning Calendar

Meeting	Item	Leader
January	Approve Fund-Raising Plan	Chair of Fund-Raising Committee
February	Hold Board Officer Elections	Chair of Nominating Committee
March	Brainstorm Potential Decisions	Board Chair
April	Evaluate Chief Executive	Chair of Personnel Committee
May	Hold Board Retreat	Board Chair
June	Discuss Marketing Plan	Chair of Marketing Committee
July	Brainstorm Potential Decisions	Board Chair
August		
September	Develop Draft Budget	Chair of Finance Committee
October	Finalize Budget	Chair of Finance Committee
November	Brainstorm Potential Decisions	Board Chair
December		

The calendar serves as a starting point that your board can customize to include the items that will enable your board to govern effectively. A blank worksheet is provided in the appendix.

Issue 7 discusses additional tools for managing meetings. For now let's consider how the ideas described in this section helped a real board. John, the board president of a literacy organization in a large Southern town, approached me for help designing the yearly board retreat. The agency was well respected in the community, was in good financial standing, and had a large client base. The board had no immediate crises to face; instead, they were seeking ways to enhance performance. In describing their challenges, John said, "Our board meetings have gotten boring. We seem to talk about routine items but never really get into how we can take our programs to the next level. There is such a need for literacy training in the city, and I know we could increase our impact."

I suggested John's board conduct a brainstorming process to stimulate their creativity and identify new areas of focus. John was excited to try the techniques. During the retreat, I led the group through a SWOT analysis and the development of an Agenda Planning Calendar. The board agreed to focus on one particular opportunity first—creating a coalition with other organizations in the city to deliver services to clients in depressed neighborhoods. Six months after the retreat, John said the discussions at the board meetings had become much more stimulating, and the coalition was thriving. The board found the brainstorming process so useful that they began using a mini-brainstorming process at the end of each meeting to help keep the Agenda Planning Calendar ever green.

Issue 2 Reflection

The following questions give you an opportunity to reflect on how *Issue 2–Operating reactively* affects your board and how the recommendations discussed in this section could help your board operate proactively.

- What insights did you gain through reading this section?

- Does your board proactively identify issues to discuss at meetings? If so, what is your process for doing this?

- Has your board ever failed to identify an issue early enough? If so, why and what was the impact on the board and the organization?

- How well do discussions at board meetings focus on agenda items? If you deviate from the agenda, why and what is the impact?

- Could any of the recommendations presented in this section help your board? If so, which ones?

CHAPTER 4
ENSURE YOU HAVE THE NECESSARY INPUTS

Correctly identifying which decision to make is not always easy for non-profit boards, as demonstrated by Issues 1 and 2, but actually ensuring your board has what it needs to make a decision presents another set of challenges.

Has your board ever made a decision with incomplete information? Several factors may explain this common situation. Board members may fail to realize that an analysis is necessary, or they may not devote time between meetings to collect the information. Even if board members collect and distribute the information, time constraints may prevent them from reviewing it. And sometimes boards do not possess certain expertise critical for making particular decisions.

This chapter describes what can happen if your board sets out to make a decision without the correct inputs, whether they are expertise (Issue 3), information (Issue 4), or full engagement (Issue 5).

Issue 3—Identify and Secure the Required Expertise

The Issue

Sometimes boards simply lack the expertise necessary to make a decision. In such a case, if a board were to seek out the needed knowledge or skills, the board could still make effective decisions. But all too often, board members are not even aware of these gaps. In other words, members "don't know what they don't know."

Most boards will find that they are just not equipped to make certain decisions without consulting others. Some common gaps include legal, accounting, marketing, or financial management expertise. Boards that proceed without filling these gaps in knowledge could encounter disastrous results. These boards fall prey to the following problem:

> *Boards sometimes make decisions that they are not qualified to make.*

One board in a small Northeastern town learned the hard way about making decisions they were not qualified to make. A former staff member threatened to sue the board, claiming back pay. Without consulting a lawyer, the board decided to resolve the issue quickly by paying what the staff member demanded. Had the board members consulted a lawyer, they would have realized the staff member's claim had no merit. Later, Harry, the board treasurer, confided in me that he felt the claim was unfounded, but some of the more vocal members had insisted on resolving the situation quickly. Consulting lawyers would have cost the board money, but it is likely they would have saved money in the long run. Even worse were the rumors that spread about the situation. Some community members criticized the board for acting rashly and setting a bad precedent. This situation damaged the board's credibility in addition to costing them money.

Addressing the Issue

Issue 3 alerts us that boards often lack the expertise necessary to make certain decisions. To make matters worse, boards often do not recognize their gaps in expertise and their need for expert help to solve certain problems. To address this issue, boards should actively evaluate their collective expertise and determine if they have adequate knowledge and experience to make a given decision. An Expertise Audit is a means to conduct such an assessment.

For major decisions, the board can use an Expertise Audit to ensure that the group possesses or can acquire the knowledge and skills necessary to make the decision. If the board determines that they lack various key knowledge and skills, they can then develop a short-term plan for gaining the expertise through consultation with outsiders. In the long term, the board can use an Expertise Audit to focus recruiting efforts. Any gaps in expertise highlight knowledge and skills the board might want to secure through recruiting new members.

Table 3 illustrates a portion of an Expertise Audit. This sample audit provides an example of a board making a decision of whether to add a high school. To complete the audit, the board considered the various types of expertise required to make the decision to add the high school. The board determined that the decision analysis would require two primary items: a projection of costs and a market analysis. Then the members evaluated themselves and decided that no member possessed the knowledge necessary to conduct a market analysis. Therefore, they developed a plan to have an outsider provide the market information.

TABLE 3. Example Expertise Audit

Expertise	Is this expertise critical, helpful, or not needed?	Why or why not? (What particular activity or analysis requires this expertise?)	Do we have this expertise? (Yes, no, or N/A)	If yes, who has it?	If no, what is our plan to get it?
Description of Decision: Should our private school add grades 9-12?					
Financial Management	Critical	A projection of costs will have to be completed to determine if the new program is feasible.	Yes	Bob	
Accounting	Helpful	This would support the previous item.	Yes	Bob	
Marketing	Critical	A market analysis will have to be conducted to determine if enrollment would be sufficient.	No		Jill will ask her friend, a marketing professor, to act as a consultant.
Public Relations/ Communication	Helpful	This would support the market analysis.	Yes	Mary	
Legal	Not Needed	Not needed at this stage in the process	N/A		
Fund-Raising	Critical	The board needs to know if there are opportunities to raise additional funds.	Yes	Mary	
Human Resources	Not Needed	Not needed at this stage in the process	N/A		
Program Related or Other	Critical	The board needs to determine if the school can deliver the curriculum.	Yes	Jim	

One board I worked with was particularly excited about the Expertise Audit. At a board retreat, the members created a list of the key decisions made over the last two years and analyzed each one to determine if they had the necessary expertise when they made the decision. In doing so, they identified several gaps in knowledge and skills and then developed a recruiting plan to fill the gaps.

Issue 3 Reflection

The following questions give you an opportunity to reflect on how *Issue 3–Lack of necessary expertise* affects your board and how the recommendations discussed in this section could help your board to identify and secure the required expertise.

- What insights did you gain through reading this section?

- Has your board ever made a decision without the appropriate expertise? If so, why and what was the impact?

- Does your board have a process for identifying the expertise needed to make a decision and then acquiring it? If so, what works well? What could be improved?

- Could any of the recommendations presented in this section help your board? If so, which ones?

Issue 4—Collect and Analyze Data

The Issue

Even when boards possess the knowledge and skills necessary to make a particular decision, they often do not set out to make the decision in an organized way. Instead, board members add key agenda items at the last minute, maybe even during the meeting, and unstructured discussions follow. This can lead to the following pitfall:

> *Board members sometimes rely on faith and not objective data to make decisions.*

Does your board fall into this trap? Many boards do. Board members tend to be passionate about their cause, and this passion can sometimes cloud their judgment when it comes to problem solving and decision making. For instance, one board suddenly lost a revenue source that accounted for 50 percent of the total revenue of the agency. During a meeting held to discuss the crisis, not one board member would commit to a specific action to address the crisis. Instead, several said, "Have faith; it will all work out." There is nothing wrong with having faith, but in the absence of proper planning, it is unlikely faith will be enough to weather such a crisis.

Consider the following example. A board wanted to rent a larger space. Such space was limited at that time, and the board found only one suitable building—with a monthly lease payment twice as much as the current payment. To make the decision to lease the building, the board quickly glanced at the financial statements and noted that the organization had $14,500 in reserve funds. The board did not consider how the decision would impact that organization six months to a year after the decision. After six months in the new building, it became obvious that the agency could not afford the increase in rent. Had board members completed a comprehensive financial analysis, they would have realized that additional funds were necessary to fund the purchase. They then could have made decisions related to finding alternative revenue or waited until they found a cheaper building.

Addressing the Issue

The preceding examples illustrate the danger of failing to research major decisions adequately. To resolve this issue, boards need to develop a process for compiling, distributing, and reviewing decision-related material and for discussing such material during meetings. This section provides guidance for effectively collecting and reviewing key decision material.

To allow sufficient time for data collection, boards should identify key decisions prior to the meeting when they will actually need to make the decisions. Table 4 illustrates an example Decision Management Checklist. This is a structured way to consider information needed to make upcoming decisions. The checklist is based on the example presented in the previous section of the board deciding whether to add a high school. A blank form is located in the appendix.

TABLE 4. Example Decision Management Checklist

Decision Management Checklist			
Describe the decision.	Should our private school add grades 9-12?		
When will the decision be made?	At the May 15 board meeting		
Describe the plan for acquiring necessary expertise, including who will do what (from Expertise Audit).	Jill will ask her friend, a marketing professor, to act as a consultant. In the future, the board will seek to recruit a member with such expertise.		
What background material is needed to make the decision?	• Existing financial statements -YES • New financial analysis -YES • Market Analysis -YES • Legal advice -NO • Other -Facility options • Other -Curriculum requirements		
Describe required material and who will gather the information.	*Description of material*	*Who will compile it?*	*By When?*
	Financial analysis using existing financial statements.	Bob and Finance Committee	May 1
	Market analysis.	Jill's friend and Mary	May 1
	Facility options.	Jeff	May 1
	Curriculum requirements.	Jim	May 1
What is the plan for distributing the information?	Bob, Mary, Jeff, and Jim will send the material to Teresa (the board chair) by May 1. Teresa will review the information and send to John (the board secretary). John will distribute material to the board members by May 5.		

To complete the checklist, the board used the results from the Expertise Audit as a starting point and then considered what additional information they would need. Before the end of the meeting, members volunteered to collect the various pieces of information and submit the information to the board chair for review and final distribution by the board secretary.

Issue 4 Reflection

The following questions give you an opportunity to reflect on how *Issue 4–Insufficient analysis of situation* affects your board and how the recommendations discussed in this section could help your board collect and analyze data more effectively.

- What insights did you gain through reading this section?

- Has your board ever made an important decision without fully analyzing the situation and necessary data? Is so, why and what was the impact on the board and the organization?

- Does your board have a process for ensuring that all relevant information is identified and collected prior to making a decision? If so, what works well? What could be improved?

- Could any of the recommendations presented in this section help your board? If so, which ones?

Issue 5—Cultivate a Fully Engaged Board

The Issue

Nonprofit boards cannot make effective decisions without fully engaged members, but most boards have at least a few members who are not as engaged as they could be. This situation presents various problems, including the following one:

> *Some board members are inaccessible between meetings or*
> *do not review information prior to meetings.*

Engagement is a state in which members invest their full energy in the work of the organization. An engaged board member will have a sense of enthusiasm for the work, exhibit focus, and go the extra mile, while a disengaged board member is likely to miss meetings, lose focus on the task at hand, and be reactive.

The following discussion describes some of the symptoms of disengagement and provides tools for addressing them. For a comprehensive discussion of the subject, *Employee Engagement: Tools for Analysis, Practice, and Competitive Advantage* by William Macey, Benjamin Schneider, Karen Barbera, and Scott Young is a good resource, and the Customized Interactions website provides specific tips and tools for ensuring you have a fully engaged board.

So how can you determine if members are disengaged? Disengaged members may show up for meetings, but they probably do not prepare beforehand and might be unresponsive to requests between meetings. In various ways this problem adversely impacts the board's ability to make effective decisions. First, boards make the best decisions when all members actively contribute their energy and ideas. If certain members are not prepared or not investing their full mental energy, their ideas are lost. Second, unprepared or unfocused members are more likely to steer the discussion off course. Third, members who are consistently unprepared can threaten the morale of the group. Finally, disengaged board members may fail to show up for meetings. If a board has a bylaw requiring a quorum to vote, then such inactivity can prevent the group from being able to make decisions.

One board consistently faced the problem of not having a quorum present because certain members would leave early or not show up at all. At most meetings the board would begin discussing a particular decision and try to reach some consensus, but those present would grow frustrated at not being able to formalize the decision. John, one of the board members, complained to me, "This is a complete waste of my time. We talk about the same thing meeting after meeting and never reach any kind of resolution." This situation caused board participation to spiral downwards as the more active members became frustrated and stopped attending meetings.

To better understand disengaged board members, let's consider why people join boards in the first place. Supporters hope a board member joins to help further the mission of the agency. But other motives might include the desire for camaraderie, career advancement, or obligation to a friend. Have any of you ever encouraged someone to join using words like "It really will not take much work. All you have to do is show up for meetings"? Unfortunately this scenario is more common than you might think.

When a person joins a board for any motive other than the desire to further the mission of the organization, there is the potential that the person will not be fully engaged. The recruiter above all should convey the seriousness of the position. This will set the tone for how the new recruit will behave in the role.

Even if individuals join because they have energy to serve the organization, they must be in an environment that supports and fosters that desire. As the previous example illustrates, engaged board members may become frustrated by lack of participation on the part of others and stop investing their full energy.

Consider another scenario. Have you ever gone above and beyond the call of duty, but your efforts were not recognized? Or, even worse, your work or decisions were criticized? I know I have, and in those situations it is difficult to continue to invest your full energy. If you do not feel appreciated and supported, or if you do not believe your effort makes a difference, you risk becoming disengaged.

I can relate personally to becoming disengaged. On one board, in the beginning I was very active in board activities and even volunteered to lead the scholarship committee. I spent hours of personal time conducting the scholarship process including reviewing scholarship applications and organizing the information for the full board to review. One year, after awarding the scholarships, an angry parent sent a letter claiming the process was unfair. That accusation hurt me deeply, because I had tried my best to be objective, and I believed the process was fair. I do not think my fellow board members realized how much the situation upset me, and in hindsight I should have been more open about my feelings. But ultimately I felt they did not offer me the emotional support I needed to deal with the situation. As a result I lost energy for working on the board, and I participated less and less until finally I had to be honest with myself and admit I was not contributing at an adequate level. It was a hard decision, but I finally resigned. It would have been easier for me to coast along, attending some meetings, providing input here and there, having a drink with fellow board members, but I knew my heart was not in it, and I needed to open the slot up for someone who would be fully engaged.

I have since rejoined the board, and this situation highlighted for me a couple of things. First, I need to be more open in expressing my concerns, and second, sometimes we have to make the hard decision to resign from our board if our situation changes and we become disengaged.

Addressing the Issue

As the previous section highlights, a fully engaged board is necessary for effective decision making. And, as my personal example reminds us, sometimes we have to make the difficult decision to resign from a board if we are not fully engaged. But often boards can take simple steps to engage members. These steps are: (1) set clear expectations when recruiting board members, (2) manage meetings in a way that respects members' time and builds relationships, and (3) create an environment that fully values members' talents and contributions. The following sections elaborate on each of these steps.

(1) Set clear expectations when recruiting new members.

Boards should periodically evaluate their recruitment methods to ensure that they facilitate the selection of fully engaged members. As noted before, individuals join boards for a variety of reasons. It is critical to select the people who are not only committed to the mission but are also willing to put in real effort and work. Thus boards should communicate clear expectations regarding the nature of the work so recruits can make an informed decision. And, instead of rushing to replace a vacant spot, boards should patiently assess candidates to ensure they will deliver to the expectations.

A good rule of thumb for estimating the minimum monthly time commitment is to include time for the monthly board meeting, a monthly committee meeting, and at least four hours of outside work to prepare for meetings and complete action items. Each specific board, however, should agree on the required time commitment. Existing members must also clearly understand what the board expects of them and evaluate whether they can do the necessary work. If a member decides he or she cannot commit the time necessary, the member should resign from the board to open up a spot for someone who can commit. Otherwise, the member compromises the board's ability to achieve its mission.

(2) Manage meetings in a way that respects members' time and builds relationships.

Have you ever been in a meeting that drags on and accomplishes little? Most of us can relate to this scenario and the resulting feelings of frustration. To ensure a highly engaged group, boards must manage meetings effectively, both from a process perspective and from a relationship perspective. This will build relationships and make good use of board member time.

For boards, meetings are the key setting for interactions. If members listen to one another and encourage open dialogue during meetings, they will build trust, strengthen relationships, and ultimately encourage more listening and open dialogue. Many of the tools discussed in this book are designed to build trust and encourage open dialogue by promoting discussion about key issues and setting clear expectations regarding how the board will operate. The Issue 7 discussion provides additional meeting practices to help achieve these ends. If members feel that the group listens and understands them, they are more likely to invest their full energy into their work.

(3) Create an environment that fully values members' talents and contributions.

A final step to ensuring a highly engaged board is to create an environment in which the board recognizes and values each individual's talents and contributions. While board members are typically driven to help the agency realize its mission, they need encouragement and recognition along the way. It also helps to ensure that board members are doing work they enjoy and that effectively utilizes the expertise they bring to the board. This will go a long way toward making members feel that their efforts are really helping the organization. Doing this well hinges on what was discussed previously: trust, open dialogue, and listening.

I have a rather humorous example of my board not understanding me very well. I had recently become vice president of my civic association. After the first meeting, the president e-mailed the meeting minutes, and to my dismay, the board had assigned me the task of submitting the tax forms. This bothered me on a couple of levels. First, we had not even discussed that task in the meetings, and, second, how could they assign someone to file taxes without asking first? The problem was, at that point our new board had not taken the time to get to know and understand one another's strengths and interests (and, in my case, weaknesses). If we had taken the time to get to know one another better, the other members would have realized that there are two tasks I always outsource: mowing the lawn and preparing taxes. We have since cleared up the confusion and now more effectively match tasks to individuals based on their strengths and interests.

In addition to understanding one another, board members should take the time to recognize their accomplishments. It is always nice to recognize each other informally, and it is a good idea for the board to schedule a special event at least once a year to that end.

To illustrate the tools discussed in this section, I will share a story about a friend of mine, Valerie, who is a board chair of a small educational agency. Valerie and I met for coffee one morning, and she exclaimed, "Lisa, this board is falling apart. What am I going to do?" She explained that two board members had recently resigned, and two were not very active. For a board of six, this was not a good situation. I suggested Valerie bring the current board together for a board retreat and focus on reenergizing the group and defining clear expectations.

During the retreat, Valerie and I had the group review the vision of the organization and list the accomplishments of the board and the broader organization over the last five years. Then we had them draft detailed job descriptions for board members, officers, and committee heads to help refocus the board members on the activities necessary for governing the organization and continuing to deliver the mission and vision. With this renewed energy and focus, the board recruited new members and used the position descriptions to set clear expectations during the interview process.

Several months later Valerie and I met for coffee again and she reflected on the experience. "Identifying our accomplishments and clarifying the expectations of board members allowed us to get two new board members who are very engaged," she said. "It also helped reenergize the current members and reminded them what was expected of them. I am much more confident now about the future of the organization."

Issue 5 Reflection

The following questions give you an opportunity to reflect on how *Issue 5-Some board members are not active or fully engaged* affects your board and how the recommendations discussed in this section could help your board cultivate a fully engaged board.

- What insights did you gain through reading this section?

- Does your board set clear expectations for board membership? If so, how?

- Are board meetings conducted in a manner that respects members' time? If not, what are the issues?

- Do you have practices in place to recognize one another and build relationships? If so, what are they?

- Could any of the recommendations presented in this section help your board? If so, which ones?

CHAPTER 5
DECIDE, FOLLOW THROUGH, AND IMPROVE

Even if boards focus on the appropriate decisions (thus, not falling prey to Issues 1 and 2) and avoid Issues 3, 4, and 5 by ensuring the board has the necessary expertise, information, and engagement of members, there is still a possibility that the decision will not be made or implemented effectively. The following sections discuss tools for identifying actions necessary to prepare for and implement decisions (Issue 6), tools for facilitating meetings in a way that enables effective decision making (Issue 7), and tools for continuous improvement (Issue 8).

Issue 6—Define and Execute Action Items

The Issue

Issue 6 is all about how well boards take the actions necessary to prepare for and implement decisions. The following is one example of Issue 6:

> *Boards often spend considerable effort making a decision but then fail to implement the decision.*

Many boards face this problem. For example, a board of a museum scheduled a special retreat to complete a strategic plan and develop an

45

action plan for the year. Board committees spent considerable time compiling the data required for the planning process. At the retreat, the board defined focus areas and developed an action plan. By the end of the retreat, the members were positive about the work they had done and were determined to implement the action plan. Unfortunately, by the next board meeting, no one had even looked at the action plan, much less taken any concrete steps toward completing the items. The board members had simply become involved in other activities and forgotten to do the work they had agreed on at the meeting. Therefore, as happens with many strategic plans, board members largely ignored it despite the work required to develop it.

So what causes lack of follow through? It may be that board members are too busy, have not fully bought into the decision, *or have simply forgotten.* I can recall meetings when I failed to write agreements down. Within a day (or even an hour), even if I tried, I could not remember the details of my commitments. Can you relate? In the next section, I describe an amazingly simple yet powerful tool. Many of you have probably used this technique, but how many can say you always use it?

Addressing the Issue

An Action Item Register is a tool that encourages the board to prepare adequately to make a decision and to implement the decisions that are made. It can also increase the effectiveness of board meetings in general. Why? Because it reminds us of what we have committed to do and makes those commitments public. This visibility helps promote accountability because most people do not want to let others down. Before or after the board makes a decision, members list the various items required to prepare for or implement it along with the individual(s) who will complete the item and the deadline. If the implementation phase is particularly complex, a group of board members might agree to meet at another time to develop the plan and an associated list of action items. In this example, the entry might be:

TABLE 5. Example Action Item Register Entry

Description of Item	Responsible Individual(s)	Complete By	Status
Develop action plan to add grades 9-12 and present to board at next meeting.	Program Committee	June 15	Open

The board should make it a practice to review the Action Item Register at the end of each meeting and add, update, or mark items complete as necessary. A key to making this successful is to have only one list and review it at every meeting, as the example illustrates.

One board was in the habit of recording action items in the minutes or in personal notes. Unfortunately, this practice was not working for them. Members would forget what they agreed to and would often find themselves noting the same item meeting after meeting because they kept forgetting it. I suggested they create an Action Item Register to organize their commitments. They tried it and were sold. Isaac, the board treasurer, exclaimed, "I cannot believe how something so basic could help us so much. We should have started doing this sooner!"

For particularly large or complex decisions that include many action items, the Action Item Register may not be enough to ensure complete implementation. In these cases, one board member can volunteer to oversee the implementation of the decision, or, in other words, be the "point" person. The point person acts as a coordinator and a champion for the implementation phase of a decision. Part of the point person's role includes ensuring that the actions in the Action Item Register reflect everything that the board needs to do to implement a particular decision. The implementation of any decision will require money, time, or both and may involve board members, staff members, or other resources. The point person helps keep the board focused on the actions necessary to implement the decision fully. The board should select the point person immediately after members make a decision, before the meeting adjourns. In addition to selecting individuals or committees to oversee implementation, the board should agree upon a process to track and report progress and document the plan in their Action Item Register.

Issue 6 Reflection

The following questions give you an opportunity to reflect on how *Issue 6-Lack of implementation* affects your board and how the recommendations discussed in this section could help your board define and execute action items more effectively.

- What insights did you gain through reading this section?

- Does your board track action items? If so, what is effective about your process? What could you do to make it even more effective?

- How well does your board implement decisions? What could your board do differently to implement decisions even more effectively?

- Could any of the recommendations presented in this section help your board? If so, which ones?

Issue 7—Facilitate Meetings Effectively

The Issue

Board meetings are where decisions are made, and they can make or break a board. Does the following statement describe your board meetings?

Board meetings last too long and accomplish little.

Board meetings often last too long because discussions veer off course and facilitators do not keep the group on task. For instance, one board regularly engaged in discussions not on the agenda. As a result, thirty minutes before the end of the meeting, the board had most of the agenda topics left to discuss, and the group continually rolled items over to the next meeting. This practice annoyed several board members who felt they were not making good use of their time because the board made few concrete decisions. This common problem affects nonprofit boards as well as groups in the corporate setting.

Addressing the Issue

The manner in which boards run their meetings has a significant impact on how effectively a board determines which decisions to make (Issues 1 and 2), ensures it has what it needs to make a decision (Issues 3, 4, and 5), and defines and executes action items (Issue 6). This section clarifies key meeting management roles, summarizes the meeting management tools presented in previous sections, and introduces new tools and practices to facilitate meetings in a way that enables effective decision making. Used together, these simple tools and practices can significantly improve your board's performance.

Understand and Clarify Meeting Roles

A first step to having effective meetings is to understand and clarify key meeting roles. The board president (or chair), chief executive, and board members all have roles to play in the meeting process, and to fully realize the benefits of the recommendations in this guide, I suggest adding a new role, the decision manager. The following paragraphs provide descriptions of each.

The board chair typically designs and leads board meetings. As meeting facilitator, the chair has responsibilities that directly impact the issues we have discussed throughout this guide. First, to design the agenda, the board chair seeks prospective agenda items from the board members and the chief executive. Examples of appropriate items might be policy discussions, proposals for new programs, and so on. To ensure a well-designed agenda, the board chair should thoughtfully consider each potential topic and ensure the topic really necessitates board action. If it does not, the board chair should direct the decision to the appropriate staff member or committee (thus avoiding Issue 1). The board chair should complete these activities before finalizing the meeting agenda and distributing it to board members. Additionally, the board chair (or board secretary) should ensure that board members, the chief executive, and other meeting attendees receive the official agenda, along with supporting materials, at least two weeks prior to the meeting so members can fully prepare (thus avoiding Issues 3, 4, and 5).

During meetings, the board chair (along with the other meeting attendees) should ensure that the group discusses agenda topics. The board may choose to have a recurring new business or round table process in which members bring up current concerns or communications. If one of the new business or round table items requires an in-depth discussion, the board chair should note it on the Agenda Planning Calendar and assign it to a future meeting. Additionally, the board chair should steer the conversation away from management concerns and toward governance and strategic issues (thus avoiding Issues 1 and 2). The last section of this *Decision Guide* contains scripts with suggested statements for board chairs to use in facilitating meetings.

The chief executive implements the policy developed by the board. Additionally, the chief executive must ensure the board has adequate information to make governance decisions and provide input during decision making. Thus the chief executive and board chair must work together to ensure that all necessary background information is gathered and used in making governance decisions.

The decision manager's role is not formal, but it can be very powerful for any board serious about implementing the recommendations discussed in this guide. The decision manager observes the board's behaviors inside and outside of meetings and, based on these observations, offers feedback and coaching to help the board avoid falling prey to the eight decision management issues. The board chair could take on the role of decision manager, but, if possible, try to find another member of the board to take on this role. Why? Because the decision manager can be a more objective observer and coach if he or she is not the one responsible for leading the meeting. In addition to acting as observer and coach, the decision manager can also organize training for the board and facilitate Decision Audits (described later in this guide) as necessary.

Facilitate to Consensus

With the correct inputs and roles in place, the board is ready to make the decision. The up front work to ensure the board is making the right decision and collecting the necessary inputs sets the board up for success. Other keys to success are to ensure open dialogue and gain consensus before finalizing the decision.

Consensus does not mean that everyone has to agree, but instead, everyone must support the decision. Sometimes, this will require members to take a course of action that is not their first choice. But in the interest of progress, the group must find the point at which they feel the decision has been fully processed and is acceptable to all members. This is a balancing act and requires discipline on the part of board members. A simple test for consensus is to go around the room and give each person a couple of minutes to express any concerns they have about the decision and whether or not they can support the decision. After doing this, the board may determine additional discussion is necessary.

After reaching a decision, the board may decide to "test" the decision with key stakeholders. Testing the decision involves meeting with affected parties, sharing details about the decision, and gathering their input about how the decision might affect them and others. This reality check provides additional information about the impact of the decision. The board can then discuss this input during another meeting before finalizing the decision.

After the decision is made, another good practice is to give each person a few minutes to articulate his or her understanding of the decision. This could uncover points of misunderstanding or disagreement that can be addressed through additional discussion before the decision is finalized. This also provides an opportunity to clarify action items and to record them in the Action Item Register. For additional tips on helping groups make decisions, see the Customized Interactions website at www.CustomizedInteractions.com.

Use Meeting Management Tools

Now, we will turn our focus to meeting management tools. Table 6 provides a summary of the tools we have discussed in previous sections:

TABLE 6. Summary of Meeting Management Tools

Decision Management Issue/Solution		Meeting Management Tool
Issue 2	Operate proactively.	Agenda Planning Calendar
Issue 3	Identify and secure the required expertise.	Expertise Audit
Issue 4	Collect and analyze data.	Decision Management Checklist
Issue 6	Define and execute action items.	Action Item Register

One additional tool that can be very helpful in designing and conducting meetings is the Agenda Template. An Agenda Template provides a road map for board meetings. Once the board agrees on a basic structure for meetings, they can create a template such as the one in table 7 developed by one of my clients. It is only partially filled out because it serves as a starting point for meeting planning. Bringing the board together to create the agenda template can help focus the group on the important elements of a meeting and ensure all members are committed to supporting the new meeting process.

TABLE 7. Example Agenda Template

Date: Time: Facilitator:		
Item	**Duration**	**Leader**
Review agenda	5 minutes	Board Chair
Review and approve treasurer report	10 minutes	Treasurer
Chief executive report	10 minutes	Chief Executive
Agenda item 1		
Agenda item 2		
Identify future agenda items	10 minutes	
Complete Decision Management Checklist	15 minutes	
Review Action Item Register	10 minutes	
Adjourn		

The meeting management tools described in this section are designed to organize meetings and save time. The board chair and the decision manager must use these tools consistently at meetings to realize their full benefit. In the beginning, using the tools may seem awkward, but after the board uses them a few times, meetings will be more efficient. Ultimately, these methods will organize the decision-making process and lead to more effective decisions.

I experienced firsthand the value of organized board processes when I joined my first board. After graduating from college, I was invited to be vice president of the local chapter of a professional association. As part of the orientation, the association provided me with bylaws, background information, role descriptions, sample meeting agendas, and all of the information I would need to be an effective board member. I have been involved in numerous organizations since, but this one stands out because this planning and orderliness showed up in all aspects of the association's operations, from how they conducted their meetings, to how they organized their programs, to how they managed their finances. Such organization can go a long way toward ensuring your nonprofit has the impact you hope it will. The meeting management practices discussed in this section are a good starting point for organizing how your board operates.

So far, this section has highlighted processes that can help make meetings more efficient and enable effective decision making, but what about relationships? The processes discussed so far help by creating structure and clear expectations, but you can employ other practices as well. Following are some practices you can use to build trust and promote understanding and open dialogue. I challenge you to try them. They are simple and can be very impactful.

- **Recognition Moment**—At the beginning of the meeting, go around the room and have each member recognize a fellow board member, staff member, or other contributor. The board may choose to invite the individual(s) to be recognized to the meeting if they are not board members. This serves to energize the group and reinforce effective behaviors.

- **Roundtable**—Boards can use this tool in a number of ways. One variation is to go around the room and have members share what they are working on or describe an area they would like the board to work on. The intent of the roundtable is to promote open dialogue and increase members' understanding of one another's challenges, ideas, and goals.

- **Call for Support**—This is a specific form of roundtable in which members ask for support. Thinking back to my example of leading the scholarship committee, if we had had such a process, I would have had a safe way to bring up my need for support in dealing with the accusation about the scholarship process.

- **Consensus Check**—This can be used when a key decision is about to be finalized. Go around the room and ask members to express any concerns they have about the decision and if they are willing to support it even if it is not their chosen course of action. Through this process, the board might determine they need additional discussion before finalizing the decision.

- **Agreements**—These are group norms or ground rules. The board can document key agreements and display the list at board meetings. For example, your board may decide you will use an Agenda Planning Calendar (or any other process or practice you agree upon). The board may also choose to document codes of conduct such as, "We will value each individual's contributions."

Issue 7 Reflection

The following questions give you an opportunity to reflect on how *Issue 7-Ineffective meeting management practices* affects your board and how the recommendations discussed in this section could help your board facilitate meetings more effectively.

- What insights did you gain through reading this section?

- Do you feel your board meetings are productive and make good use of your time? Why or why not?

- How does your board reach consensus on decisions? What is effective about the process? What could be improved?

- What meeting facilitation techniques do you use? Which work particularly well and why?

- Could any of the recommendations presented in this section help your board? If so, which ones?

Issue 8—Improve Continuously

The Issue

The problems described in the previous sections may happen repeatedly if boards have not developed a means to evaluate and improve the effectiveness of their decision making. In other words, boards (and other groups) tend not to take the time to identify and learn from their mistakes. Thus, it should not surprise you that:

Boards make the same mistakes more than once.

For instance, one board routinely made financial decisions using financial reports board members did not completely understand. As a result, they continued to agree to expenses that they thought were prudent, but in reality, the organization could not afford. At one point, when the funds in the operating account were noticeably low, the board members realized there was a problem. When they finally probed deeper into the finances with the help of an expert, they discovered that a record-keeping mistake made several years earlier masked a larger problem.

So what issues led to this situation? Issue 3 certainly had a role in this because the members of this board lacked strong financial expertise. They had to bring in an expert to help identify the problem and then correct the financial records. As a result of this experience, the board developed plans to fill the gap in financial expertise. Issue 4 also played a role because the board members did not collect sufficient information to make the financial decisions within their responsibility. Some of the other issues also likely contributed to this situation, but the key point here is that developing an ongoing process to evaluate and improve decision making and meeting management can help avoid problems such as this.

Addressing the Issue

Decision Audits are a means to evaluate and improve upon board decision-making processes. They help groups refine their decision practices and learn what works and what does not work. Decision Audits are not conducted for the purpose of sanctioning people for their mistakes, but instead they are purely learning tools. Groups must make this clear up front to ensure all board members are comfortable with the process.

The board should conduct a Decision Audit at least once a year and after implementing a major decision. What constitutes a major decision depends on the agency and the board. Some examples of major decisions might be the addition or cancellation of a program or service, the decision to acquire a new facility, the decision to hire a chief executive, or the decision to make a large purchase. A decision should be audited soon after the board implements it so members can remember the specifics of the decision-making process. The board should also conduct periodic evaluations throughout the implementation process to make sure that everything is on track and that they did not overlook anything during the decision-making stage. The decision manager or the board chair can initiate and facilitate the Decision Audits. Table 8 provides an example of a Decision Audit Worksheet completed by the board discussed at the beginning of this section. A blank worksheet is located in the appendix.

TABLE 8. Example Decision Audit Worksheet

Describe a recent key decision: We decided whether to fund a new program.		
Describe the outcome of the decision: Several months after starting the program, the funds in our operating account were lower than expected. After reviewing the finances, we realized we had problems with our financial reports.		
Analyze the Decision-Making Process		
Issue 1—Clarify roles.		
Does the board clearly understand their roles and responsibilities?	YES☑	NO☐
Was this decision a responsibility of the board?	YES☑	NO☐
Issue 2—Operate proactively.		
Was the Agenda Planning Calendar used to plan key topics for the year?	YES☐	NO☑
Were periodic brainstorming sessions conducted to identify potential critical decisions?	YES☐	NO☑
Were discussions focused on necessary issues and decisions?	YES☑	NO☐
Was this decision necessary?	YES☑	NO☐
Issue 3—Identify and secure the required expertise.		
Was an Expertise Audit completed prior to making this decision?	YES☐	NO☑
Did the board have or find the expertise necessary to make the above decision?	YES☐	NO☑
Issue 4—Collect and analyze data.		
Does the board regularly collect the data necessary to make decisions?	YES☐	NO☑
Was the Decision Management Checklist completed for this decision?	YES☐	NO☑
Did members follow through on the plan and review data beforehand?	YES☐	NO☑
Issue 5—Cultivate a fully engaged board.		
Are board members active?	YES☑	NO☐
Are expectations for board membership clear?	YES☐	NO☑
Do board members feel that their time and effort is appreciated?	YES☑	NO☐
Issue 6—Define and execute action items.		
Does the board regularly use the Action Item Register?	YES☐	NO☑
Was this decision properly implemented?	YES☑	NO☐
Issue 7—Facilitate meetings effectively.		
Are board meetings run effectively in general?	YES☑	NO☐
Was the time spent on this decision appropriate?	YES☐	NO☑
Issue 8—Improve continuously.		
Does the board have a plan for conducting periodic Decision Audits?	YES☐	NO☑
If a Decision Audit has been conducted, did the board implement a Decision Enhancement Plan?	YES☑ NO☐ N/A ☐	

The first step to conducting a Decision Audit using the Decision Audit Worksheet is to consider how well the board avoided each of the decision management issues. The questions in the worksheet direct the board to consider this by asking questions about each issue. After the board answers each question by checking yes or no, the board then considers all the questions in which no was the answer. These are the areas for growth and continuous improvement. For instance, if the board answered no to the question *Does the board regularly use the Action Item Register?*, they might consider what impact that had on the implementation of the decision and perhaps decide to begin using the Action Item Register.

The board should not ignore the yes answers. These indicate strengths in the board's decision-making process. For instance, if the board answered yes to the question *Are board members active?*, they might want to congratulate themselves and consider how to ensure activity remains at a high level. The Decision Enhancement Plan offers an organized means to identify specific actions or plans to address decision management issues and recognize and enhance strengths. Table 9 provides an example plan based on the audit in Table 8, and a blank worksheet is located in the appendix.

TABLE 9. Example Decision Enhancement Plan

Issue	Change Review your Decision Audit Worksheet. Reflect on the items you answered NO. Identify actions the board will take to strengthen these areas.	Continue Doing Review your Decision Audit Worksheet. Reflect on the items you answered YES. Reflect on why you are strong in these areas.
ISSUE 1 Clarify roles.		Our board has a good understanding of roles and responsibilities, and we focus on governance decisions.
ISSUE 2 Operate proactively.		
ISSUE 3 Identify and secure the required expertise.	We do not have adequate financial expertise, so we are recruiting a new member with that exerptise.	
ISSUE 4 Collect and analyze data.	We will use the Decision Management Checklist to collect all of the information necessary to make a decision.	
ISSUE 5 Cultivate a fully engaged board.		We feel engaged and appreciated. The issue with the finances helped strengthen our board because we worked together to solve the problem.
ISSUE 6 Define and execute action items.	This audit helped us realize we need to be more disciplined in recording and tracking action items.	
ISSUE 7 Facilitate meetings effectively.		
ISSUE 8 Improve continuously.	We will continue conducting periodic Decision Audits.	

Issue 8 Reflection

The following questions give you an opportunity to reflect on how *Issue 8-No decision audits* affects your board and how the recommendations discussed in this section could help your board improve continuously.

- What insights did you gain through reading this section?

- Has a decision your board made ever turned out badly? Did your board discuss the situation openly? Why or why not?

- Does your board have a process for evaluating board performance and identifying areas for improvement? If so, what works well? What could be improved?

- Could any of the recommendations presented in this section help your board? If so, which ones?

Summary of Decision Management Solutions

Table 10 summarizes the eight issues and tools and strategies you can use to avoid them. The next section provides practical advice on how to implement the recommendations presented in this guide.

TABLE 10. Summary of the Eight Decision Management Issues

Issue	Description of Issue	How Can This Issue be Addressed?
ISSUE 1 Lack of role clarity	Board members have not reached a common understanding concerning what they should do and what the staff should do.	**Clarify roles.** 1. Ensure the board does not neglect governance activities. 2. Discuss and agree upon board and staff roles and responsibilities. 3. Document role descriptions.
ISSUE 2 Operating reactively	Boards are sometimes blindsided because they have failed to discuss or identify a problem early enough.	**Operate proactively.** 1. Conduct periodic brainstorming sessions to identify decisions that should be made. 2. Use the Agenda Planning Calendar to plan key topics for the year. 3. Keep discussions on track through the use of effective meeting management practices.
ISSUE 3 Lack of necessary expertise	Boards sometimes make decisions that they are not qualified to make.	**Identify and secure the required expertise.** 1. Complete an Expertise Audit prior to making major decisions. 2. Rely on outsiders when necessary. 3. Ensure that the board has the necessary expertise through recruitment.
ISSUE 4 Insufficient analysis of situation	Board members sometimes rely on faith and not objective data to make decisions.	**Collect and analyze data.** 1. Identify key decisions prior to the meeting when the decision will be discussed. 2. Complete the Decision Management Checklist to develop a plan for gathering and organizing the information.
ISSUE 5 Some board members are not active or fully engaged	Some board members are inaccessible between meetings or do not review information prior to meetings.	**Cultivate a fully engaged board.** 1. Set clear expectations for board membership. 2. Ensure potential board members are willing to meet the expectations. 3. Respect board members' time and recognize their efforts.
ISSUE 6 Lack of implementation	Boards often spend considerable effort making a decision but then fail to implement the decision.	**Define and execute action items.** 1. Use the Action Item Register to record items. 2. Review and update the Action Item Register at each meeting.
ISSUE 7 Ineffective meeting management practices	Board meetings last too long or accomplish little.	**Facilitate meetings effectively.** 1. Use the meeting management tools presented in the *Decision Guide*. 2. Facilitate meetings effectively.
ISSUE 8 No decision audits	Boards make the same mistakes more than once.	**Improve continuously.** Conduct periodic Decision Audits.

CHAPTER 6
IMPLEMENTATION TIPS

So how can you put the *Decision Guide* into practice? Here are some tips. First (and you have probably already done this!), review the *Decision Guide* from the perspective of your board. What is your board struggling with? Which tools would be particularly valuable to address your challenges? Then, propose an agenda item for an upcoming board meeting and describe the *Decision Guide*—the process and how it might benefit your board. After you make a case for using the tools, if the board members decide to initiate the process, it is time to decide how and when. Here are some items to consider as you develop your specific plan:

- **What do you hope to achieve through implementing this process?**

  Make sure you have clearly defined your goals and how you hope to improve your board's performance. Reflect on the following questions: In what areas would you like to strengthen your board? What issues are you facing that you hope to address? Clearly articulating your goals will focus the group and help make the case for the time required for implementing the process.

- **Will your board use specific tools or implement the process in its entirety?**

Ideally, you should introduce the process during a full-day board retreat when your members can reflect on their past performance and discuss how to use the tools to improve. Another option is to start slowly, possibly introducing one new tool each quarter. Your board may already be using some of the tools presented in this guide. In this case, it would be useful to reflect on how effectively you are using a given tool and identify any areas for continuous improvement.

- **When do you want to meet as a group to work through the tools?**
  The tools described in this guide can be presented in their entirety during a board retreat or in a series of shorter meetings.

- **Who will be the decision manager?**
  A decision manager (maybe you!) is critical to implement the process. The decision manager should be someone who is excited about the process and will remind and encourage other board members to participate actively in the process. With board meetings typically occurring only once a month, members can easily forget or lose interest in new information. The decision manager should remind and encourage the board members to practice the recommendations presented in the *Decision Guide*.

- **How will you customize the process?**
  The board must customize the process as they gain insight into what works and what does not. I recommend the board dedi-

cate one meeting per year for a Decision Audit and to update the written decision-making process.

- **Will you seek advice or support in implementing this process?** Having an external facilitator helps you define your goals, customize the process, and facilitate group interactions. You may contact Customized Interactions to discuss options for external consultation and facilitation of the *Decision Guide* process.

CHAPTER 7
ADDITIONAL RESOURCES FOR DECISION MAKING

The following are some additional ideas and resources that boards can use to help improve decision making and meeting management.

The Power of Scripts

Scripts are statements you can use to keep meetings on track and help implement the recommendations presented in this guide. You do not have to read the statement verbatim, but it can provide insight into how you might address certain situations. As you learn new techniques, having scripts in mind can keep you on track until the new behaviors become second nature. Table 11 lists scripts that the board chair, decision manager, and others can use to address the various decision management issues. These are only some of the statements that might be useful. Your board will likely be able to identify others that would be helpful and relevant to your challenges.

TABLE 11. Decision Management Scripts

	Examples of Statements
ISSUE 1 Clarify roles.	"Is this a management or governance decision?" "This is a decision for the staff. Let's note it and inform the appropriate staff member after the meeting."
ISSUE 2 Operate proactively.	"This topic is not on the agenda. I will note it, and we can add it to the agenda of an upcoming meeting." "This is an important topic, but it should be discussed in a committee meeting."
ISSUE 3 Identify and secure the required expertise.	"Do we really have the expertise necessary to make this decision?" "This is a major decision. We should evaluate what additional expertise might be necessary to make it by completing an Expertise Audit."
ISSUE 4 Collect and analyze data.	"This is an important decision, but we have not had a chance to thoroughly analyze the issue. Therefore, let's develop a plan for collecting the information now and discuss the decision at the next meeting."
ISSUE 5 Cultivate a fully engaged board.	"As you recruit new members, remember to let them know what we expect of them in terms of meeting attendance and work outside of meetings."
ISSUE 6 Define and execute action items.	"Before we leave today, let's develop a plan for making this decision a reality." "This is a key action necessary to implement the decision. Who will volunteer to complete this item by the next meeting?"
ISSUE 7 Facilitate meetings effectively.	"Let's stick to the agenda so we can finish our meeting on time. I will note your concern, and we can add it to next month's agenda." "Before we leave today, let's determine what next month's key agenda items will be so we will have a chance to gather the necessary information."
ISSUE 8 Improve continuously.	"That was a major decision. Let's conduct a Decision Audit at the next meeting."

So do scripts really work? Consider the following example. One board I worked with was in the habit of micromanaging. (Remember Issue 1?) I suggested the board keep the question "Is this a management or governance decision?" in mind and be ready to ask it if anyone began discussing items that were the staff's responsibility. The board found this particularly useful and even took it a step further by writing the statement on a piece of flip-chart paper and taping it to the wall of their meeting room as a constant reminder.

Brainstorming Techniques

Proactively selecting decisions to make (Issue 2) requires brainstorming ideas and options. Using an organized process can help you generate quality ideas while avoiding analysis paralysis or needless destructive conflict. Below is an outline of the steps.

1) Start by generating ideas. Go around the room one or two times, giving each participant a chance to contribute one idea. If you are using the SWOT framework, first ask board members to give strengths. After recording all of the strengths, ask for weaknesses, and so on. Have a meeting facilitator (preferably a person not involved in the brainstorming process) capture the ideas on a dry erase board, flip chart, or computer (if you use a computer, make sure to project it on a screen so the group can see the ideas). Throughout the idea-generation phase, do not discuss or judge the ideas. Simply record them.

2) After allowing time for the free flow of ideas, you can start to narrow down the list. This is the stage when participants can explain or clarify their ideas. First, consider if any of the ideas are duplicates or similar. Combine duplicate or similar ideas if all participants agree. Second, decide which ideas do not align with the mission of the organization and strike them from the list.

3) Next, prioritize and select ideas. Divide the number of ideas by seven to determine the number of selections each participant will have. For example, if the group presents twenty-one ideas, each person may choose three. Voting can proceed in various ways. The following are two possibilities:

- The facilitator reads each idea, and participants vote by raising their hands (as many times as they have votes). The facilitator records the number of votes each idea receives.
- Participants get markers or stickers. Then they go up to the dry erase board or flip chart and indicate their votes by placing a check mark or a sticker beside their selections.

4) The facilitator can then count the votes and process the ideas. If an idea receives a low number of votes, the person who presented the idea (or anyone else) may take three minutes to speak in support of the idea so it may remain on the list. Items that receive a low number of votes may be taken off the list with agreement from the group. Items that receive a high number of votes but face opposition by an individual may be modified. The aim is to gain agreement from all participants that they will support the potential decisions even if they are not a participant's chosen course of action.

Organizations

BoardSource provides practical information, tools, best practices, and training for boards of nonprofit organizations. The BoardSource website (www.boardsource.org) provides links to various topic papers and answers to questions in a variety of areas, including meeting management, decision making, and board and staff roles and responsibilities.

Customized Interactions provides resources to enable boards to make decisions that are more effective. You may contact Customized Interactions if you would like a consultant to work with your board to implement the process discussed in this book. The Customized

Interactions website (www.CustomizedInteractions.com) provides contact information, tips for decision making, as well as other resources for boards including a Strategic Planning Guide.

Books

Decision Management, by Frank Yates, provides a comprehensive discussion of decision management issues faced by corporate boards and teams.

Nonprofit Boards: What to Do and How to Do It, and *Effective Meetings: Improving Group Decision Making* both by John Tropman, offer suggestions that can be used to increase the effectiveness of nonprofit board decision making and meetings.

APPENDIX
DECISION GUIDE TOOLBOX

This section provides a summary of all of the tools presented in this guide and worksheets and templates you may use. For electronic versions of these worksheets and templates, see the Customized Interactions website at www.CustomizedInteractions.com.

Issue 1—Clarify Roles

Use the Role Clarification Reflection to evaluate past decisions to determine if the board is making the right decisions.

TABLE A1. Role Clarification Reflection

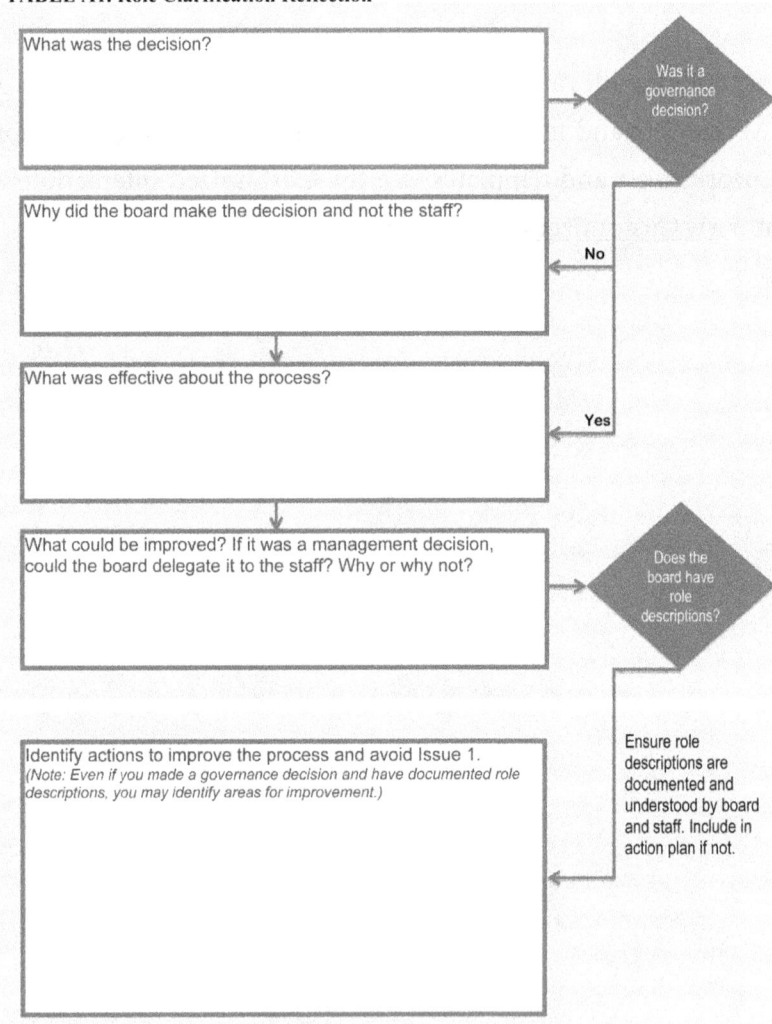

What was the decision?

Was it a governance decision?

Why did the board make the decision and not the staff?

No

What was effective about the process?

Yes

What could be improved? If it was a management decision, could the board delegate it to the staff? Why or why not?

Does the board have role descriptions?

Identify actions to improve the process and avoid Issue 1. (Note: Even if you made a governance decision and have documented role descriptions, you may identify areas for improvement.)

Ensure role descriptions are documented and understood by board and staff. Include in action plan if not.

Issue 2—Operate Proactively

Use the Agenda Planning Calendar, along with a brainstorming process, to design and conduct effective board meetings. Include major activities and topics to discuss at future board meetings. At each board meeting, update it to include new agenda items identified through the course of the meeting and delete any irrelevant items.

TABLE A2. Agenda Planning Calendar

Meeting	Item	Leader
January		
February		
March		
April		
May		
June		
July		
August		
September		
October		
November		
December		

Issue 3—Identify and Secure the Required Expertise

Use the Expertise Audit to ensure that the board possesses or can acquire the knowledge and skills necessary to make a major decision.

TABLE A3. Expertise Audit

	Expertise Audit				
Description of Decision:					
	ANALYSIS OF DECISION		BOARD SELF-EVALUATION		
Expertise	This expertise is critical, helpful, or not needed.	Why or why not? (What particular activity or analysis requires this expertise?)	Do we have this expertise? (Yes, no, N/A)	If yes, who has it?	If no, what is our plan to get it?
Financial Management					
Accounting					
Marketing					
Public Relations/ Communi- cation					
Legal					
Fund-Raising					
Human Resources					
Other and/or Program- Related Expertise					

Issue 4—Collect and Analyze Data

Use the Decision Management Checklist to identify information needed to make upcoming decisions and to develop a plan for collecting the information.

TABLE A4. Decision Management Checklist

Decision Management Checklist			
Describe the decision.			
When will the decision be made?			
Describe the plan for acquiring necessary expertise, including who will do what (from Expertise Audit).			
What background material is needed to make the decision?	• Existing financial statements • New financial analysis • Market analysis • Legal advice • Other		
Describe required material and who will gather the information.	*Description of material*	*Who will compile it?*	*By when?*
What is the plan for distributing the information?			

Issue 5—Cultivate a Fully Engaged Board

Ensure members of your board are fully engaged and feel appreciated by doing the following:

- Set clear expectations when recruiting board members.
- Manage meetings in a way that respects members' time and builds relationships.
- Create an environment that fully values members' talents and contributions.

Many of the recommendations and tools presented in this guide will help cultivate a fully engaged board. For additional tips, visit the Customized Interactions website, www.CustomizedInteractions.com.

Issue 6—Define and Execute Action Items

Use the Action Item Register at every meeting to track progress and hold one another accountable. Table A5 provides one version. The Customized Interactions website, www.CustomizedInteractions.com, provides additional templates.

TABLE A5. Action Item Register

Description of Item	Responsible Individual(s)	Complete By	Status

Issue 7—Facilitate Meetings Effectively

Use the tools presented in this guide to drive effective meeting management and decision making. Key items to remember are:

1) Understand and clarify key meeting roles.
2) Test for consensus before finalizing a decision.
3) Use the Agenda Planning Calendar (presented in Issue 2) and Action Item Register (presented in Issue 6) regularly.
4) Use the Expertise Audit (presented in Issue 3) and Decision Management Checklist (presented in Issue 4) when preparing to make key decisions.
5) Use an Agenda Template to help plan meetings. Table A6 provides a template. Additional templates are provided on the Customized Interactions website at www.CustomizedInteractions.com.

TABLE A6. Agenda Template

Item	Duration	Leader
Date:		
Time:		
Facilitator:		
Review agenda		
Review and approve treasurer report		
Chief executive report		
Agenda item 1		
Agenda item 2		
Identify future agenda items		
Review Action Item Register		
Adjourn		

Issue 8—Improve Continuously

Use the Decision Audit to conduct periodic evaluations of your board's decision-making processes (see worksheet on next page).

TABLE A7. Decision Audit Worksheet

Describe a recent key decision:	
Describe the outcome of the decision:	
Analyze the Decision-Making Process	
Issue 1—Clarify roles.	
Does the board clearly understand their roles and responsibilities?	YES☐ NO☐
Was this decision a responsibility of the board?	YES☐ NO☐
Issue 2—Operate proactively.	
Was the Agenda Planning Calendar used to plan key topics for the year?	YES☐ NO☐
Were periodic brainstorming sessions conducted to identify potential critical decisions?	YES☐ NO☐
Were discussions focused on necessary issues and decisions?	YES☐ NO☐
Was this decision necessary?	YES☐ NO☐
Issue 3—Identify and secure the required expertise.	
Was an Expertise Audit completed prior to making this decision?	YES☐ NO☐
Did the board have or find the expertise necessary to make the above decision?	YES☐ NO☐
Issue 4—Collect and analyze data.	
Does the board regularly collect the data necessary to make decisions?	YES☐ NO☐
Was the Decision Management Checklist completed for this decision?	YES☐ NO☐
Did members follow through on the plan and review data beforehand?	YES☐ NO☐
Issue 5—Cultivate a fully engaged board.	
Are board members active?	YES☐ NO☐
Are expectations for board membership clear?	YES☐ NO☐
Do board members feel that their time and effort is appreciated?	YES☐ NO☐
Issue 6—Define and execute action items.	
Does the board regularly use the Action Item Register?	YES☐ NO☐
Was this decision properly implemented?	YES☐ NO☐
Issue 7—Facilitate meetings effectively.	
Are board meetings run effectively in general?	YES☐ NO☐
Was the time spent on this decision appropriate?	YES☐ NO☐
Issue 8—Improve continuously.	
Does the board have a plan for conducting periodic Decision Audits?	YES☐ NO☐
If a Decision Audit has been conducted, did the board implement a Decision Enhancement Plan?	YES☐ NO☐ N/A☐

Issue 8—Improve Continuously

Use the Decision Enhancement Plan to identify specific actions to address issues and recognize strengths.

TABLE A8. Decision Enhancement Plan

Issue	Change	Continue Doing
	Review your Decision Audit Worksheet. Reflect on the items you answered NO. Identify actions the board will take to strengthen these areas.	Review your Decision Audit Worksheet. Reflect on the items you answered YES. Reflect on why you are strong in these areas.
ISSUE 1 Clarify roles.		
ISSUE 2 Operate proactively.		
ISSUE 3 Identify and secure the required expertise.		
ISSUE 4 Collect and analyze data.		
ISSUE 5 Cultivate a fully engaged board.		
ISSUE 6 Define and execute action items.		
ISSUE 7 Facilitate meetings effectively.		
ISSUE 8 Improve continuously.		

BIBLIOGRAPHY

Ingram, R. T. *Ten Basic Responsibilities of Nonprofit Boards*. 2nd ed. Washington DC: BoardSource, 2009.

Macey, W. H., B. Schneider, K. Barbera, and S. Young. *Employee Engagement: Tools for Analysis, Practice, and Competitive Advantage*. Chichester, England: Wiley-Blackwell, 2009.

Tropman, J. E. *Effective Meetings: Improving Group Decision Making*. Thousand Oaks, CA: SAGE Publications, Inc., 1996.

Tropman, J. E., and E. J. Tropman. *Nonprofit Boards: What to Do and How to Do It*. Washington DC: CWLA Press, 1999.

Yates, J. F. *Decision Management*. San Francisco: Jossey-Bass, 2003.

ACKNOWLEDGMENTS

This book is the result of the support and influence of many people in my life.

First, I thank my friends who provided inspiration and support. A heartfelt thanks to Theresa Medoff for listening to countless updates of my progress and encouraging me through moments of frustration.

Thanks to Gabrielle Townsend for sharing her experiences of working in the nonprofit sector and giving me confidence that my work and ideas will help nonprofit boards.

And to Elaine Kempski who left the corporate world to follow her dream and calling in life. She has been an inspiration to me.

Thanks to my colleagues at DuPont who provided encouragement and many interesting insights.

A special thanks to Professor Frank Yates for providing the catalyst for this book. My work with him gave me the initial ideas for the book and the confidence to persevere.

I thank the many board and staff members of the nonprofits I have worked with over the years. I learned much from those experiences.

And to the Kirkwood Highway Starbucks crew for keeping me supplied with early morning coffee as I wrote this book.

I thank my family for their support and encouragement. My father is always available and able to answer my writing questions. My mother has provided many useful ideas and insights from her experience in the nonprofit sector.

A special thanks to Kim Champion for providing support in my journey and reminding me to always look to God for direction and validation.

Finally, and most importantly, I thank God for creating me and always being with me. My faith is my most cherished gift in life.

ABOUT THE AUTHOR

Lisa Dahmus earned a Chemical Engineering degree from the University of Texas, Austin, and then worked as a team building facilitator for Dow Chemical. This was followed by an MBA from the University of Michigan and two years in Management PhD programs, where she studied Organizational Behavior.

While in graduate school, the author taught Management and Organizational Behavior to undergraduates and pursued research on organizational learning and change, team effectiveness, and nonprofit board development.

After graduate school, she joined DuPont, where she was certified as a Six Sigma Black Belt and is a Change Management Consultant providing organizational effectiveness training and consulting to corporate teams.

Throughout her career and studies, the author has worked with nonprofit boards designing and delivering training to fit their unique needs and based on these experiences has further developed her processes by which boards can increase their effectiveness.

ABOUT CUSTOMIZED INTERACTIONS

Lisa Dahmus is the President and Founder of Customized Interactions, a consulting practice focused on increasing board effectiveness. The eight issues described in this book are the basis for the offerings provided by Customized Interactions. For more information visit www. CustomizedInteractions.com.

www.ingramcontent.com/pod-product-compliance
Lightning Source LLC
Chambersburg PA
CBHW060629210326
41520CB00010B/1528